Influential Latinos

EVA LONGORIA

Actress, Activist, and Entrepreneur

Richard Worth

Enslow Publishing
101 W. 23rd Street
Suite 240
New York, NY 10011
USA
enslow.com

Published in 2016 by Enslow Publishing, LLC
101 W. 23rd Street, Suite 240, New York, NY 10011

Library of Congress Cataloging-in-Publication Data
Worth, Richard.
Eva Longoria : actress, activist, and entrepreneur / Richard Worth.
    pages cm. — (Influential Latinos)
Includes bibliographical references and index.
Summary: "Discusses the life and work of Eva Longoria"— Provided by publisher.
ISBN 978-0-7660-6993-0
1. Longoria, Eva, 1975—Juvenile literature. 2. Actors—United States—Biography—Juvenile literature. I. Title.
PN2287.L6325W68 2015
791.4302'8092—dc23
[B]
                        2015012778

Printed in the United States of America

To Our Readers: We have done our best to make sure all Web site addresses in this book were active and appropriate when we went to press. However, the author and the publisher have no control over and assume no liability for the material available on those Web sites or on any Web sites they may link to. Any comments or suggestions can be sent by e-mail to customerservice@enslow.com.

Photo Credits: AF archive/Alamy, pp. 32, 40, 60, 63; Albert L. Ortega/WireImage/Getty Images, p. 54; Alberto E. Rodriguez/Getty Images Entertainment/Getty Images, p. 4; Alexander Tamargo/Getty Images Entertainment/Getty Images, p. 80; Arun Nevader/WireImage/Getty Images, p. 31; Barry King/WireImage/Getty Images, p., 23; Central Press/Hulton Archive/Getty Images, p. 78; Chris Greenberg/Getty Images Entertainment/Getty Images, p. 89; CLEMENS BILAN/AFP/Getty Images, p. 52; Cliff Lipson/CBS Photo Archive/Getty Images, p. 29; D Dipasupil/FilmMagic/Getty Images, p. 106; Everett Collection/Shutterstock.com, p. 1; Frederick M. Brown/Getty Images Entertainment/Getty Images, pp. 6, 72; Gabriel Olsen/Getty Images Entertainment/Getty Images, p. 66 Gary Miller/FilmMagic/Getty Images, p. 26; Jeff Kravitz/Film Magic/Getty Images, p. 34; Jeff Schear/Getty Images Entertainment/Getty Images, p. 68; John Moore/Getty Images News/Getty Images, p. 76; Michael Caulfield/WireImage/Getty Images, p. 84; Michael Tran/FilmMagic/Getty Images, p. 48; Mirek Towski/FilmMagic/Getty Images, p. 45; Noel Vasquez/Getty Images Entertainment/Getty Images, p. 112; Peter Ptschelinzew/Lonely Planet Images/Getty Images, p. 12; Photos 12/Alamy, pp. 38, 46; Stephen Lovekin/Getty Images Entertainment/Getty Images, p. 74; Steve Granitz/WireImage/Getty Images, p. 19; ROBYN BECK/AFP/GettyImages, p. 86; Ron Galella/WireImage/Ron Galella Collection/Getty Images, p. 92; Vantagnews.co.uk/Ipx/AP Images, p. 101; Victor Chavez/WireImage/Getty Images, p. 97; ZUMA Press, Inc./Alamy, p. 25; Wenn Ltd/Alamy, pp. 58, 108.

Cover Credit: Everett Collection/Shutterstock.com (Eva Longoria).

Contents

Eva Longoria was named Philanthropist of the Year by the *Hollywood Reporter* in 2009.

Chapter 1

A CELEBRATION

For Eva Longoria, it was an evening of celebration. But the talented actress and star of *Desperate Housewives* was not being honored because she had won another television award, nor was she being recognized for producing another outstanding film. In November 2009, Longoria was named Philanthropist of the Year by the *Hollywood Reporter,* and she was being honored for her achievements. After the awards ceremony, the newspaper planned to hold a private reception in Longoria's honor.

"I've never met a more conscientious and socially aware young, energetic talent," explained the *Hollywood Reporter* publisher Eric Mika. "Eva's efforts on behalf of the causes near and dear to here are herculean. She pours her free time and energy into raising millions of dollars for charitable missions that make a difference in the Latino community and other humanitarian organizations."[1]

Longoria poses with children from PADRES, just one of many charitable causes the actress and philanthropist supports.

PADRES

In 2003, for example, Longoria began a long association with PADRES Contra El Cancer (Parents Against Cancer) serving as their spokeswoman. Her involvement with PADRES began because Eva had visited children with cancer in local hospitals and wanted to do something that might help them and their parents. On November 1, 2014, Longoria hosted a PADRES fund-raising event that honored Keck Hospital at the University of Southern California for its work with young cancer patients.

"As the father of a child who is a cancer survivor," explained Scott Evans, head of the hospital, "I understand the unique needs of children suffering from the disease. We applaud PADRES Contra El Cancer's mission to support young cancer patients and their families, and we are honored to be recognized by such a compassionate organization."[2]

The celebration lasted for an entire weekend and included a silent auction, an awards presentation, and musical performances.

Eva's Heroes

In addition to her work with PADRES, Longoria is also a founder of Eva's Heroes, located in San Antonio, Texas. This organization, started in 2006, is dedicated to helping young people ages 14 and older who have special needs. Every year, the organization holds a series of fund-raising events that are designed to help carry out the four principles of Eva's Heroes. These are *interact, grow, learn,* and *love.*

These principles are realized through a variety of after-school programs such as Thanksgiving Week activities, Winter Holiday activities, Spring Break Week Activities, and Summer Enrichment activities. Young people learn how to improve their abilities to interact with others, live more independently, and enhance their teamwork skills.

The Harvest

However, Longoria's philanthropic work in the community did not end after being honored by the *Hollywood Reporter* in 2009 for PADRES and Eva's Heroes. In 2011, Longoria also produced a documentary film, called *The Harvest,* which describes the lives of migrant children. As the actress/producer explained, *The Harvest* exposes the blatant exploitation of children who work in U.S. agriculture and feed America. It's a sad fact that those who feed the most well-fed nation in the world often go to bed hungry."[3]

There are an estimated 400,000 of these children who work in the agricultural fields, planting and harvesting crops, for 14 hours every day of the week. Wages are very low, and farm workers are exposed to toxic pesticides that can undermine their health.

The documentary tells the story of several children such as Zulema Lopez, age 12, who heads out to the onion fields of south Texas with her family before sunup each morning. Because she must work every day, Zulema has very little time to do her schoolwork. At times, she

Longoria produced *The Harvest*, a documentary that follows the lives of child migrant workers.

becomes very frustrated. "I stop picking crops," she explained, "and just lock myself in the truck for hours and I think, 'Maybe I should stop this and do my work for school.'"[4] But she continues to follow her family from Florida to Texas trying to earn enough money to survive. Unfortunately, migrant families average only $17,500 annually in income.

The documentary was directed by U. Roberto Romano, who has directed other films on child labor. "You see the hardscrabble life," he explained. "You see the insecurity, you see how difficult it is. You see the uncertainty, and it just makes you wonder that in America today we still allow this to happen to our own children."[5]

In 2011, Longoria and others lobbied for a bill that was introduced into the U.S. Congress to change child labor laws. Known as the Children's Act for Responsible Employment, (CARE), it is designed to prevent children ages 10 to 13 from doing agricultural work. Because the children must travel regularly, they have little time for school. As Longoria put it, "Many of the children are stuck in a cycle of poverty because of their obligations in the field and to their families, and many of these children are not able to break that cycle because they don't have the chance or opportunity."[6]

Eva Longoria recognizes that the same thing could have happened to her. It is one of the reasons she has been so highly motivated to utilize her success, her acting fame, and her financial resources to give back to the community.

Chapter 2

CORPUS CHRISTI ROOTS

E va Jacqueline Longoria was born on March 15, 1975 in Corpus Christi, Texas. But her ancestry stretches all the way back to Medieval Spain.

Texas History

The city of Corpus Christi (Spanish for Body of Christ) lies in south Texas along the coast of the Gulf of Mexico. With a population of over 300,000, the city boasts one of the largest ports in the United States. Cargo ships and tankers carrying wheat, oil, and other products leave the port daily for destinations in many parts of the world. The city also has a mild climate with beautiful beaches, especially those on Padre Island, with the longest barrier beaches in the United States.

While the area had been home to Native Americans for centuries, the first European to visit the Texas coast was probably the Spanish explorer Alvar Nuñez Cabeza

San Jacinto Monument commemorates the location where Texas achieved independence from Mexico.

de Vaca. He was shipwrecked on its shores during the sixteenth century. The local Museum of Science and History held an exhibit in 2013, showing the remains of another Spanish vessel that had been shipwrecked on the coast, possibly similar to the one that carried de Vaca to the New World.

De Vaca was an intrepid adventurer who visited numerous areas along the North American coast, and in Central and South America. While in Texas, he traveled among the Native Americans, bringing healing medicines to the sick and winning for himself a reputation for kindness that lasted long after he had departed.[1]

In 1519, another Spanish explorer Alonzo Alvarez de Pineda landed along the coast and explored the area. Over the next three centuries, settlers from Mexico followed de Pineda and moved into the Southwest, including New Mexico, Arizona, and Texas. Accompanying them were Spanish priests who established missions among the Native Americans, and Mexican soldiers who built presidios, or forts, to protect the area. By the early 1800s, this Mexican empire stretched for hundreds and hundreds of miles. Its capital was located in Santa Fe, New Mexico.

However, the Mexican empire faced two large threats. One came from the Native American tribes, such as the Apache and Comanche, who did not want their hunting grounds disturbed by white settlers. And the second threat came from 300,000 American settlers who lived west of the Appalachian Mountain range and wanted to move into the Mexican Empire.

Eventually, they were successful. American settlers came to Texas, including Stephen Austin, who established a settlement along the Brazos River that runs through south Texas in 1822. From 1838 to 1839, Colonel Henry Lawrence Kinney, another colonizer like Austin, set up a trading post on the present site of Corpus Christi, calling it Kinney's Ranch. Some of the settlers became cattle ranchers, while others established cotton plantations and brought their slaves into the area.

By that time, the Texians, as they called themselves, had decided that they no longer wanted to remain part of the Mexican empire. In 1836, they had declared their independence. The Mexican Army, led by General Antonio de Santa Anna, greatly outnumbered the Texian militias and initially put down the rebellion with victories at the Alamo in San Antonio and Goliad. But a Texian army commanded by General Sam Houston later defeated and captured Santa Anna at the Battle of San Jacinto. The Mexican general agreed to let Texas become independent in return for his freedom.

Calling itself the Lone Star Republic, Texas remained independent until 1845, when it joined the United States. Two years later, during the Mexican War, the United States acquired most of the rest of the Mexican empire in the Southwest.

Tracing Her Roots

Over the next half century, many Mexicans continued living in Texas, especially in the south around Corpus Christi. In addition, Mexican immigrants moved into Texas from south of the border. One of these was Ponciano Longoria, Eva Longoria's great, great grandfather. The Ponciano family had roots that stretched back to the Age of the Explorers.

Born in Mexico in 1853, soon after the end of the Mexican War, Ponciano and his family came north into Texas in 1859. Ponciano later married Rita de Villarreal, who had also emigrated from Mexico. She had been born there in 1864 and came to Texas as a two-year-old. .

Ponciano's father, Juan Longoria, had already bought about 4,400 acres (1781 hectares) of land from Rita's father, Don Gregorio Villarreal, in 1873. More acreage was added to the Longoria landholdings by Ponciano, and Rita inherited additional property from her father. Altogether they owned more than 5,000 acres (2023 hectares), which Ponciano called Santa Rita Ranch, after his wife.[2]

For his PBS series, *Faces of America*, Professor Henry Louis Gates Jr. traced the ancestry of many well-known Americans. Among them was Eva Longoria, for whom he traced her ancestry in Texas. As Gates explained in his interview with Longoria, Lorenzo Longoria, a distant ancestor, sailed from Spain to the New World in 1603, the same year that the Jamestown colony was founded in Virginia. Years later, another ancestor was given a land grant of about 4,000 acres (1619 hectares) in Mexico by the King of Spain. The Longorias owned this land for about a hundred years.

Mexicans like Ponciano then came north into Texas to continue the tradition of ranching. But there they often encountered opposition from Anglo settlers who had moved into Texas. While Mexican-American ranchers were accustomed to let their cattle run on the open range between ranches, the Anglo ranchers enclosed their property with barbed wire, keeping out the cattle of the Mexican-American ranchers. If these ranchers protested, the Anglos often hired expensive lawyers to sue the Mexican Americans. If this was not entirely successful, the Anglos relied on the local police force, the Texas Rangers, to brutally enforce rough justice against the Mexican Americans.

One of these Anglo ranchers owned the giant King Ranch in south Texas, founded by Richard King in the 1800s. Ponciano Longoria found himself in a dispute with the King family and went up to his ranch in 1913. There he was stabbed to death by one of King's ranch hands. Before his death, Ponciano and his wife Rita had ten children, although four had died by 1900. One of them, Antonio, was later killed by Texas Rangers, according to Gates, as he was trying to defend his land and the future of his family.[3] As Eva Longoria put it, when her aunt was asked to use one word to describe the history of the Longoria family in Texas, she said, "survival."[4]

Facing Discrimination

For more than half of the twentieth century, the years before Eva Longoria's birth, Mexican Americans in Texas faced strong discrimination at the hands of Anglos who controlled the local government. Mexican-American children were forced to attend segregated schools, which were not as good as those attended by Anglo children. Teachers were not properly trained, desks and blackboards were also missing in most classrooms. By this time, many Mexican-American parents had lost their land and found themselves working in the agricultural fields owned by Anglos. Often their children worked alongside their parents, with little time to attend school—much like the children in *The Harvest*.

Eventually, Mexican Americans formed organizations designed to end this inequality. One of these was the League of United Latin American Citizens (LULAC), which won an important court case in Texas that outlawed discrimination in the 1940s. Another organization, the G.I. Forum, was founded in Corpus Christi. This group lobbied for the rights of Mexican-American soldiers who had fought in World War II. These men had been denied an opportunity for a higher education, one granted to other veterans under the G.I. Bill of Rights.

However, it took several decades for discrimination to end. The civil rights movement for African Americans led by Dr. Martin Luther King Jr. in the 1960s not only helped end discrimination for blacks but also for

Hispanic Americans. Throughout the Southwest, many went to the polls and voted for their own candidates at the local and state level in states like New Mexico and Texas. In the 1960s, Henry Gonzalez was elected a

Five Facts about Corpus Christi

1. The city has the fifth-largest port in the United States.
2. Corpus Christi has more species of birds than any other city in the United States.
3. The major industries in Corpus Christi are agriculture and tourism.
4. The King Ranch is the oldest working cattle ranch in the United States.
5. Corpus Christi has never received a snowfall that was deeper than 5 inches (13 cm).

congressman from San Antonio. In 1974, a year before Eva's birth, Jerry Apodaca was elected governor of New Mexico and Raul Castro, governor of Arizona.

Growing Up in Corpus Christi

Born in 1975, Eva was the youngest of four daughters of Ella Eva Mireles and her husband Enrique Longoria Jr. She has three sisters: Elizabeth Judina, Emily Jeannette, and Esmeralda Josephina. Her sister Elizabeth (Liza) suffered from a physical disability that threatened to take her life. But she survived with care from her sisters and her mother, who became a special education teacher as a way of helping her. Eventually, Liza went to high school,

Eva Longoria grew up in a loving, tight-knit family that included her parents and three sisters.

like the rest of her sisters. The entire family, including Eva, took great pride in Liza's success.[5]

As Eva was growing up during the 1970s, Corpus Christi was struck by Tropical Storm Amelia in 1978. This was one of many giant storms and hurricanes that struck the area during the 20th century.

In 2006, Eva took viewers of *The Oprah Winfrey Show* to her family's farm in Texas. They were not well-to-do, she said. Among her sisters, she was known as *La prieta fea*, which means the "ugly, dark one." However, Eva still hoped to someday become a fashion model. She sent her pictures to a modeling agency, but the agency was not interested in her, she admitted to Oprah.

Longoria attended Baker Middle School and Roy Miller High School, where she became a cheerleader. She also worked at a local Wendy's restaurant while attending high school. After graduation, Eva went to Texas A&M University in Kingsville, Texas, where she majored in kinesiology—the study of physical movement. This major might have enabled Longoria to have a career in physical therapy and sports medicine. But chance would lead her elsewhere.

Chapter 3

THE BIG BREAK

Texas A&M, Kingsville, is located southwest of Corpus Christi in a town named after Richard King. The beautiful campus is home to the first university to offer a doctoral program in bilingual education. It also offers majors in agriculture, engineering, music, and various sciences. Over 8,000 students attend the university, most of them from South Texas, and more than 60 percent of the students are Hispanic. The university has been praised by *U.S. News and World Report* for its Environmental Engineering program and is ranked among the top 100 national universities.

Eva Longoria joined many others students majoring in the sciences and graduated with a bachelor of science (BS) degree. While attending the university, she also fulfilled her interest in acting by winning roles in college theatrical productions. Meanwhile, she returned to her hometown to compete in the Miss Corpus Christi beauty pageant. The "ugly, dark one" had grown into a beautiful woman, outshining the other competitors in every category of the event, and eventually she was crowned Miss Corpus Christi, 1998.

In 1998, when Longoria handed over her crown to a new Miss Corpus Christi, she said, "It has helped me grow a lot as an individual." "I feel sad because this year has been filled with so many memories. At the same time I feel joy for the next queen to be….I hope she uses the opportunities to her benefit as I did."

A Learning Experience

Eva told Mike Bratten, reporter with the *Corpus Christi Caller-Times* newspaper that she had learned a lot after being crowned Miss Corpus Christi. "My communications skills have improved because I've talked to people from elementary school students to the mayor of Corpus Christi," she explained. "It has helped me grow as an individual," she added. "It's been very hard for me to say no to anyone because I want to help everybody and I want to leave a great impression on them. I would like to be seen as a beautiful person—more on the inside and out."[1]

Breaking into the Entertainment Industry

As a result of her victory in the beauty pageant, Longoria won a personal development course with the Infinity Modeling and Talent Agency, as well as other opportunities in Hollywood. These included an advertisement for Sears department stores and her

Longoria developed poise and communication skils that served her well in her modeling career and in life.

selection to appear on the cover of a Harlequin romance novel. She also auditioned for parts in several movies and television programs, as well as for commercials for McDonald's and Pepsi.[2]

Longoria explained that after graduating from college, she wanted to study for a Master's Degree in marketing, with a specialty in exercise science. "To me, health is your greatest wealth. You can't function as a productive individual if you're not healthy." Longoria added: "I live out of a suitcase because I've been traveling so much but I always find time for exercise. I even exercise in my hotel room. I started kick boxing recently."[3]

Winning a beauty pageant has opened a door to success for many young women. It has led to modeling careers, film contracts, and starring roles in television. But once the door has opened, a beauty pageant winner must know how to take advantage of all the opportunities that come her way. This takes intelligence, poise, and the ability to make good decisions—knowing what jobs to take and which ones to turn down.

Eva's success as Miss Corpus Christi also enabled her to enter the Miss Texas USA pageant in 1998. In the pageant, contestants are judged in three areas: the interview competition, swimsuit competition, and evening gown competition. In her interview, Eva had to demonstrate self-confidence as well as poise and charm as she answered questions from the host of the pageant. The swimsuit competition required her to show off her

Longoria poses with actor José Solano at the Imagen Awards in 1998.
The Imagen Awards recognize the accomplishments of Latinos in the
entertainment industry.

Thanks to her education, beauty, grace, and self-confidence, Eva Longoria was ready to begin an acting career.

physical fitness, face, and figure. And finally Eva had to select an evening gown that best enhanced her beauty.

While Eva did not win the event, her career in television and movies had already been launched. In the years ahead, she would become one of the most familiar faces on the screen.

Chapter 4

TELEVISION ACTRESS

Eva's beauty pageant appearances ended with the Miss USA competition. But about the same time she met Executive Producer Gary Ghiaey during a political event in Los Angeles. The producer asked her to appear on a segment of his television show, *L.A. in a Day* in 1999. From this job, Longoria landed an appearance on the popular TV series, *Beverly Hills, 90210* in 2000.

This long-running series began airing in October 1990 and ran for the next ten years on the Fox Network. The program, named after one of the zip codes in Beverly Hills, describes the experiences of two teenage twins, Brandon and Brenda Walsh, when their family left Minneapolis and moved to Beverly Hills. Following hit ratings, when Fox ran new episodes of the show during July and August, 1991—a time when most networks showed reruns—the program was eventually named one of the Best School Shows of All Time.

The series did not shy away from dealing with controversial subjects like teenage suicide and pregnancy, AIDS, and abortion. *Beverly Hills, 90210* also turned several of its actors, like Jason Priestly, Luke Perry, Jennie Garth, and Tori Spelling into television stars.

This was not lost on Eva Longoria. So, when she was offered a role on one of the weekly episodes in 2000, she accepted. It was a small, cameo role as a flight attendant. Eva was stopped after her flight arrived in an airport and asked by a male actor whether she had seen a man named Eddie Waitke.

"The flight was completely full," Longoria answered. "I barely remember my name." She suggested that another flight attendant might be more helpful. And that was it; Longoria walked off the set. Unfortunately, she never appeared on the series again, although it ran for a total of over 290 episodes as its main characters went to high school, attended college, and entered adulthood.

Other Roles Follow

Following *Beverly Hills, 90210,* Eva landed another cameo role, this time on the long-running daytime soap opera, *General Hospital.* She played a double for Brenda Barrett, a character thought to have died when her car went over a cliff. Another actor on the show was Tyler Christopher, who played Nikolas Cassadine.

Born in Joliet, Illinois in 1972, Tyler Christopher Baker is the son of Jimi-Ann, a Choctaw Native American, and Jim Baker, a member of the Seneca tribe. After attending college at Ohio Wesleyan for a couple of

Longoria got her start on daytime soap operas, including a cameo on *General Hospital* and a regular role on *The Young and the Restless*.

years, Tyler went to Hollywood, changed his name, and began an acting career. In 1996, he started appearing in *General Hospital*, continuing to appear in the soap opera for the next two decades.

After Christopher and Longoria met, they dated for a while and eventually eloped to Las Vegas, where they were married in January 2002. However, as both of them tried to pursue their separate careers, they eventually put too much stress on their relationship, which fell apart two years later. The couple divorced in January 2004.

Longoria later said that she had been too young for marriage. But she added, "In a divorce, no matter the relationship, it's still the death of something. And you have to mourn it....And then you're like, 'Coulda, shoulda, woulda?' And I like to say, 'I'm going to mourn over it, and it's never going to come back.' Then you move on."[1]

Asked if she might marry a second time, Longoria said, "I married before when I was too young and eloped to Vegas. This time I'd love to have an engagement and a big wedding and do it properly....You don't know who you are when you're in your twenties so I think it's really difficult to be selfless."[2]

The Young and the Restless

While married to Tyler Christopher, Longoria landed a starring, regular role in the daytime soap *The Young and the Restless*. From 2001 to 2003, she played the part of Isabella Brana, one of the program's femme fatales. Brana was portrayed as an angry, vindictive character, and Longoria recalled that it was a challenging part to play.

After joining the cast, Longoria's character began to have an affair with Paul Williams and later became pregnant with his child. This infuriated Paul's wife, Christine. However, Isabella Brana was not really in love with Paul and instead wanted his friend Michael Baldwin, with whom she also began to have an affair. Isabella later told Paul that she was carrying his child and he resumed his relationship with her.

However, the couple was unable to get along with each other, and Paul eventually went back to his wife, Christine. Isabella was so upset that she tried to

Longoria married *General Hospital* star Tyler Christopher in 2002. She blames their youth for the failure of the marriage.

Longoria starred with Ed O'Neill in the network crime drama *Dragnet*. This experience was her biggest role yet.

kill Christine, who was saved by Paul. Isabella was arrested and committed to a clinic for the mentally ill, disappearing from the show. Longoria told the *Los Angeles Daily News* that while she had been paid very little for the show, it had helped her to "better things."[3]

After being written out of *The Young and the Restless*, Longoria appeared for two years in the police show *Dragnet,* on which she played the role of Detective Gloria Duran. *Dragnet* had originally aired on television in the 1950s. The program was created by actor Jack Webb, who starred as Sergeant Joe Friday. The show was designed to portray the effectiveness of the L.A. Police Department in hunting down and arresting criminals. Although Webb died in 1982, the program was revived in 2003.

Longoria appeared along with Ed O'Neill, as Sergeant Friday, and his partner, Frank Smith, played by Ethan Embry. Longoria was in a series of regular episodes that dealt with such crimes as the death of a salesman, who was shot and fell out a window, the rampage of a serial killer, and the search for a missing teenager. This experience would make Longoria even more comfortable in front of the camera, exploring new characters, and getting to know people in Hollywood.

Longoria and her *Desperate Housewives* castmates had no idea how successful their show would become.

Chapter 5

STARDOM

D*ragnet* lasted only two seasons. It proved to be an unsuccessful attempt to revive a TV formula that had been popular in the 1950s, but seemed very dated in the 21st century. Eva had played a backup role to the two male leading actors. Her part seemed one-dimensional, not very demanding, and appeared not to stretch her acting abilities.

All of this changed in 2004, when she was cast in a leading role on the primetime soap opera, *Desperate Housewives,* created by Executive Producer Marc Cherry. Later Eva would look back and say, "I am so grateful for what the show has given me! And a special thanks to Marc Cherry who forever changed my life."[1]

She was right. *Desperate Housewives* made Eva Longoria a television star recognized around the world.

The Success of *Desperate Housewives*

Desperate Housewives began appearing on the ABC Network at 9PM Eastern time on October 3, 2004, a

Sunday evening. The premiere was watched by over 21 million viewers, reaching 30 million by the end of the first season.[2] Beginning on American television, the series, which ran to 2012, was eventually seen annually by more than 100 million viewers around the world.

Cherry was a successful television producer who had created several television comedies, including *The Golden Girls,* a long-running hit about a group of older women. *Housewives* was shot on a set at Universal Studios in Hollywood. Many television programs are shot on sets like this one, if the series always occurs in the same place and doesn't require on-location shooting in a variety of settings.

Desperate Housewives was set on fictional "Wisteria Lane," in a seemingly perfect, affluent suburb. But one of these housewives, Mary Alice Young, played by actress Brenda Strong, had not enjoyed a perfect life. For reasons not understood by her friends, she had committed suicide. Now, after her death, Mary Alice narrates the program, taking us into the lives of her neighbors in this American suburb.

Four housewives formed the nucleus of the series. There was Susan Mayer, a divorced mother, played by actress Teri Hatcher. Lynette Scavo, played by Felicity Huffman, was a mother and had been a successful career woman. Marcia Cross played the third housewife, Bree Van de Kamp, who was struggling in an unhappy marriage. And then there was Eva Longoria's character:

Gabrielle Solis, a former fashion model married to businessman Carlos Solis (Ricardo Antonio Chavira).

The Character of Gabrielle Solis

Gabrielle Solis—the youngest of the four housewives—had made her way up the ladder of success to become a well-known fashion model in New York City. After meeting Carlos, a wealthy entrepreneur, Gabrielle realized that he offered more than she could ever find in a career. He was also very attracted to her, and after a few dates, he proposed marriage.

Following their wedding, Carlos moved Gabrielle to a beautiful home on Wisteria Lane, surrounded by all of the material possessions that money could buy. But, after moving to the suburbs, Carlos spent most of his time at work and Gabrielle became bored with her empty life.[3] This boredom led her to begin an affair with a high school student, John, who had been hired as the gardener.

Gabrielle and John continued having their affair, although the couple was almost caught by Carlos, who returned home early one day from his work. Carlos later told his mother, Juanita, that he thought his wife was having an affair, and Juanita agreed to spend more time with her daughter-in-law to catch her with John, the young gardener.

Meanwhile Gabrielle and the other housewives threw a party in honor of the late Mary Alice Young. John attended the party, where he and Gabrielle were spied by a nine-year-old girl from the neighborhood as

Ricardo Antonio Chavira and Eva Longoria played Carlos and Gabrielle Solis, a couple with a tempestuous marriage.

the couple embraced. To ensure her silence, the girl then began blackmailing Gabrielle.

Later in the first season, Juanita was accidentally struck by a car that put her into the hospital. Meanwhile, John had begun a relationship with someone else in the neighborhood, angering Gabrielle, who finally ended her affair with him. In order to deal with her boredom, Gabrielle went back to work as a model, but she could not find work as a supermodel any longer. Instead, she had to accept a job at a mattress company. After being fired for talking back to customers, Gabrielle later worked for a cosmetics firm.

As the series approached the end of the first season, Gabrielle's husband, Carlos, was sent to prison for illegally employing an immigrant. Meanwhile, although Gaby did not want children, Carlos did and tampered with her birth control pills. As a result, she found herself pregnant. The steamy role played by Eva Longoria in *Desperate Housewives*, especially Gaby's affair with a teenage gardener, made her an instantly recognizable star. She began appearing on the covers of national magazines. Nevertheless, her grandmother was not completely happy with Eva's success. She "disapprove[d] of Eva's *Desperate Housewives* sex scenes," according to *People* magazine, "yelling at her after watching" them.[4]

Longoria got the chance to show off both dramatic and comic skills playing the materialistic but big-hearted Gaby.

Chapter 6

THE SUCCESS OF DESPERATE HOUSEWIVES

The success of *Desperate Housewives* came not only from the strength of its scripts but also from the skills of its four primary actors. On one level, the series was an evening soap opera. Each week, Gaby dealt with a new episode in her love life and her marriage to Carlos. Bree tried even harder to become the perfect housewife and mother, while overlooking the needs of her husband. Lynette had to cope with the frustrations and lack of fulfillment she felt trying to raise four children with little or no help from her husband. While Susan tried to raise a daughter following her divorce as she also searched for a new man in her life.

However, this was only one level at which the show operated. At another level *Desperate Housewives* was a slick comedy about four women who seemingly had everything but believed they had almost nothing at all.

And this put them into some very funny situations. Gaby's love life with the teenage gardener, John, while Carlos was busy pursuing millions in the financial industry led her into some very humorous escapades. In the pilot for the series, for example, she rushes home from a party to mow the lawn in her evening gown so Carlos won't find out that John was busy with Gaby while he was supposed to be taking care of the lawn.

Meanwhile, Bree and her family are sitting at their dinner table while her children are busy criticizing the fact that every supper she prepares has to be a perfect gourmet meal instead of pork and beans out of a can, like their friends often get from their moms. Lynette runs into an old friend from work in the supermarket who asks her whether she is enjoying motherhood with four little children. As her three little boys are busy pushing a shopping cart furiously up and down the aisles running into customers, Lynette smiles and tells her friend that she thinks motherhood is the most wonderful job she could ever have.

The Housewives' Opening Seasons

During the first few seasons, *Desperate Housewives* tried to present enough interesting plot twists to keep viewers coming back for more and more. After Bree's husband has been murdered, she tries to deal with being a single mother, although alcoholism almost defeats her. She eventually marries someone who may have been involved with a recently unearthed dead body. Lynette

Keys to Writing a Successful Soap Opera

Don't reinvent the wheel. Examine the approach of successful soap operas, currently running and in the past, and model your approach on theirs.

Create a half dozen or so main characters. Give each one a different set of character traits, making sure that every main role is believable but also interesting for potential viewers.

Make sure to lay out a sequence over a year's episodes for each character, showing how they interact and relate to each other. Make the plots as interesting as possible and involve as many of the main characters as possible.

Write your first script, indicating dialogue and interactions on one side of the page and visuals on the other. These visuals should include settings, actions, etc.

Throughout all of the episodes, keep each character consistent with his/her personality. No one should step out of character and make decisions or deliver dialogue that seems inconsistent with their personalities.

To keep viewers interested, introduce mysterious new characters, extreme actions from time to time, romantic scenes, and a cliffhanger in the final episode.

returns to her career in advertising, but then develops cancer.

Gaby wants to renew her relationship with John, the gardener, until she sees him going inside the house of another woman in the neighborhood. In a funny scene, Gaby becomes so angry, she gets a set of hedge clippers and destroys the woman's rose bushes. Meanwhile,

Gaby's husband, Carlos, is finally released from prison. But the couple divorces, and Gaby marries Fairview's new mayor, Victor Lang. Nevertheless, she and Carlos have not forgotten each other and they begin an affair after Gaby's marriage.

During these early seasons, *Desperate Housewives* and its main actors were recognized for their outstanding work with numerous awards from the entertainment world. In 2006, Eva Longoria was nominated for a Golden Globe Award for Best Performance by an Actress in a Television Series, Comedy, or Musical for her role as Gabrielle Solis. The Golden Globes have traditionally honored actors, directors, and writers in television. That same year, Longoria was named Person of the Year and received an ALMA Award (American Latino Media Arts Award). The ALMAs had begun in 1987 and recognized American Latino contributions in film, television and music. This was Eva's second ALMA. Her first had come in 2002 for her role in *The Young and the Restless*.

In 2007, Longoria was recognized with a People's Choice Award, which is voted by television viewers, as Favorite Female TV Star. In 2005 and again in 2006, the cast of *Desperate Housewives* won the Screen Actors Guild award for Outstanding Performance by an Ensemble in a Comedy Series. In 2006, Longoria was also recognized with the Teen Choice Award for "Breakout Performance" by a female—an award given by teen viewers. Longoria loved being a part of this hit show, and she loved stretching her acting muscles playing a character so

Longoria was recognized for her stellar work on *Desperate Housewives* with several nominations and wins.

Desperate Housewives focused on a group of women with seemingly perfect suburban lives.

different from herself. She told one interviewer, "I'd love to be a housewife. I'm very domesticated, much more like Bree than Gabrielle. I clean all the time, and I sewed all the curtains in my house. I love cooking and making amazing Mexican food; everybody loves my tortilla soup."[1]

Chapter 7

A PUBLIC AND A PRIVATE LIFE

Eva Longoria's success in *Desperate Housewives* brought other parts her way, as Hollywood producers tried to capitalize on her stardom for their own films. In 2006, Eva played the role of a rookie Secret Service Agent in *The Sentinel*, a film starring Michael Douglas and Kiefer Sutherland.

In an interview with CBS News, Longoria was asked whether she enjoyed being in the film. "It was great," she said. "I was star struck … [every time] I heard my name linked with Michael Douglas and Kiefer Sutherland."[1]

Eva also talked about her role in *Desperate Housewives*, and its impact on her family. "We grew up with soaps," she explained. "We couldn't afford to go to the movies." She added that her family was "proud" she was a part of the show.[2]

Eva Longoria met basketball star Tony Parker in 2004. The two had much in common, including their love of sports.

Tony Parker

Meanwhile, Eva's private life began to take a new turn. In 2004, she had met Tony Parker, a point guard for the San Antonio Spurs professional basketball team. "When I first saw him, he took my breath away," Longoria recalled.[3]

Parker was born in Bruges, Belgium on May 17, 1982. He was seven years younger than Eva Longoria. Tony grew up primarily in France, where his father, Tony Sr., played professional basketball. A graduate of Loyola University, Tony Sr. had left the United States to play basketball in Europe. There he met model Pamela Firestone and married her. Besides Tony, the couple also had two other sons, Terrence and Pierre.

During the summers, the Parker family flew back to the United States and spent time with Tony's grandparents in Chicago. There he learned to play basketball and watched the man who became his idol, Michael Jordan of the Chicago Bulls. After returning to Europe, Tony played point guard with junior teams in France and won a most valuable player award while competing in a junior tournament in 1997. In 2001, Parker, only 19, was the star of the French team that competed in the European Championships, averaging over 25 points per game.

Sitting in the stands and closely watching the games was R.C. Buford, assistant General Manager for the San Antonio Spurs. In the 2001 NBA draft, the spurs selected Parker to play point guard for them. In his first season with the Spurs, Parker scored an average of over nine points per game and was selected by the NBA to play on the All-Rookie First Team.

The following season, Tony helped the Spurs into the playoffs, where he averaged more than 17 points per game against the Seattle Supersonics. Then in 2003, Parker helped the Spurs defeat the New Jersey Nets for the NBA championship. Hoping to add another championship during the next season, the Spurs were disappointed when they lost to the Los Angeles Lakers. But in the following seasons, the Spurs and Tony Parker added two more NBA titles to their list of accomplishments.[4]

Parker and Longoria

Many of Parker's finest games were attended by Eva Longoria. In turn, he stood by her side at Hollywood galas, and the couple appeared together in a variety of popular magazines. In November 2006, Eva and Tony became engaged. They were married less than a year later on July 6, 2007 in Paris city hall, followed by a wedding at a Catholic Church located nearby.

Unfortunately, Eva and Tony were only married for a short time. In 2010, the couple decided to divorce. Eva later explained that Tony had been having a romantic relationship with another woman, and she had discovered her messages to him on his cell phone.[5] In an interview with USA Today, Longoria said that she had asked herself, "Am I not sexy enough? Am I not pretty enough? Am I not smart enough?" But then she added "In so many of those questions, I immediately stopped

Longoria's New House

Meanwhile, Eva had been building a magnificent home in San Antonio, Texas, where the couple lived after their marriage. The sprawling mansion boasted five bedrooms, five bathrooms, an indoor basketball court where Tony could practice, a swimming pool, and a gym. A large open living room featured long arched windows that provided beautiful natural lighting, and the couple cooked in a spacious modern kitchen.[6]

and go, 'No, don't start doing that.' Because you can get stuck in that cycle and you can carry on to other things."[7]

Life Mirrors Art

In a way, Eva's personal life seemed to mirror the role she played in *Desperate Housewives*. As she returned for her fifth season in 2008, the series had jumped ahead by five years. By this time Gaby is raising two daughters, one of whom she believes might have a weight problem. Meanwhile, Carlos has been dealing with blindness, which he eventually overcomes. But this creates anxiety for Gabrielle, who fears that he might not find her as attractive as before. In a series of humorous scenes, the already curvy Gaby thinks she must take extraordinary steps to improve her looks.

Desperate Housewives regularly featured cameo appearances by guest stars, like the comedian Bob

Longoria waved to fans in Paris before her civil ceremony to Parker. Unfortunately, the marriage was short-lived.

Newhart and supermodel Heidi Klum. For example, in the sixth season, Gaby returns to the modeling agency where she used to work. There she runs into Klum, who Gaby has always claimed is a dear friend of hers. But Klum does not respond like a friend. That's because years earlier Gaby had taped toiled paper to the bottom of one of Heidi's shoes, which she wore while walking the runway at an important fashion show in New York. Gaby simply regarded it as a practical joke, but Klum claims it cost her an important job.

In the same program, Gaby also runs into supermodel Paulina Porizkova, another person she claims as a friend. But Paulina's recollection of their relationship is quite different: while she helped Gaby getting started, Gaby repaid her help by being unpleasant.

Gaby seems to be living in a dream world, trying to convince herself that she is more important than she really is. While expecting to find happiness with Carlos and all her expensive possessions on Wisteria Lane, she is disappointed. Unfortunately, Eva had found similar disappointment in her own marriage.

In its first season, *Desperate Housewives* earned six Emmy Awards, the most prestigious television award.

Chapter 8

GABRIELLE SOLIS: DESPERATE HOUSEWIFE

The story of Gabrielle Solis and the other desperate housewives who lived on Wisteria Lane continued for eight seasons, going off the air in 2012. Gradually, in the later seasons, ratings for the programs declined, overtaken by other shows that appeared in the same time slot. Averaging almost 24 million viewers for each episode in its first year, making it among the most watched programs on television, the series declined to about 8 million in its final season, 35th place for total number of viewers.[1]

As played by Eva Longoria, the character Gabrielle Solis also experienced her ups and downs. From a modeling career in New York City, Gaby went to Wisteria Lane in Fairview as the wife of successful businessman Carlos Solis. At first, Gaby thought she had found happiness but later confessed to her gardener and teenage lover that perhaps she had looked for it in the wrong place. Soon her financial stability was jeopardized after her husband was arrested and put in jail for selling products made by slave labor. Eventually, he was released with the help of a beautiful nun, Sister Mary Bernard. Jealous of Sister Mary's relationship with Carlos, Gabrielle schemed to have her transferred out of state—a scheme that eventually succeeded. Unfortunately for Gaby, her marriage to Carlos continued to decline and the couple finally divorced in the third season of the series. That same year, she married Victor Lang, a local politician, but soon began an affair with her former husband that opens the fourth year of the series. When Victor discovered the affair, he took Gabrielle for a cruise on his boat. She believed that Victor wanted to murder her but she pushed him into the water and immediately sailed away. Victor survived, but after trying to murder Carlos, he died in a storm.

In the fifth season, the series had moved ahead by five years. Carlos, who lost his eyesight in the same storm that killed Victor, eventually regained it. Together he and Gaby have been raising two daughters, Juanita and Celia. Unfortunately, Gabrielle had very little interest in being a mom or in dealing with the childhood problems faced by her daughters.

During the final two seasons, Gabrielle's violent stepfather, Alejandro, who had raped Gaby as a child,

The Colors of Gabrielle Solis

Tom Walsh, the production designer for *Desperate Housewives* explained that the paint colors for the homes of each of the main characters had to reflect each one's personality. For example, the exterior of Gabrielle's house is yellow with white trim. Inside, where every room—living room, bathrooms, even Gabrielle's walk-in closet—is large, Walsh said that "We're basically using color to help tell the story. We're doing a commercial for the suburbs."[2] Gabrielle's colors are gray for the foyer and soft pumpkin for the living room, "to show her passionate side." Then there are variations on warm orange colors to "hint at her spicy nature and even her marital infidelity...."[3]

began stalking her. Gaby threatened her stepfather with a gun and he disappeared, only to return to attack her at home. But Carlos arrived just in time to stop Alejandro and kill him. Soon afterward, Bree, Susan, and Lynette arrived for a dinner party, but, instead, agreed to help Carlos and Gaby bury Alejandro.

In the final season, Bree was charged with killing Alejandro. But, after a trial, a jury found her not guilty. Meanwhile, Gaby had taken a job as a personal shopper to help with her family's financial struggles. But she continually flirted with male customers to make sales, angering Carlos. As the series ended, the major characters had moved away from Wisteria Lane. Gabrielle started an online shopping service, which led to an offer in

In the fifth season, the show jumped ahead by five years, and suddenly Carlos and Gaby were raising two daughters.

Hollywood to host a show on television. Gabrielle and Carlos left Wisteria Lane for a new home in Los Angeles.

The Finale

The final show of the series was a two-hour program on May 13, 2012. "It's that satisfying ending you want in a show that's been running eight years," Longoria said.[4] The actors received their scripts a month in advance. Marcia Cross, who played Bree in the series, recalled that she began to look over the script after putting her 5-year old twins to bed. "Evenings are a blur," she said. "But once the girls were asleep I read it on my computer because there was all this anticipation."[5]

Eventually, the cast met to go over their lines together. "It was a crying fest," Longoria said. "I couldn't get through my dialogue." Later, Longoria sat with Marcia Cross and Felicity Huffman "crying, hugging, and reminiscing." Cross recalled, "It was a sweet, private moment for us."[6]

The four stars had also done very well financially as a result of the series. By the final season, each of them was being paid $325,000 per show.[7] The success of *Desperate Housewives* would also lead to other lucrative opportunities. In the years ahead, Eva would be able to use the series as a launching pad to other roles and other achievements.

During a break in shooting *Desperate Housewives*, Longoria costarred in the 2006 movie, *The Sentinel*.

Chapter 9

EVA'S FILMS

Eva's success on *Desperate Housewives* had catapulted the actress into the top ranks of stardom. It also led to a variety of offers to appear in Hollywood movies. While none of these films became blockbusters, they enabled Longoria to hone her skills as an actress and to increase her exposure among the millions of fans who had watched her on television.

Even before *Housewives* aired on television, Eva was appearing in films. In 2004, she starred in a film called *Senorita Justice*. This low-budget film features actress Yancy Mendia as lawyer Anna Rios who investigates the murder of her brother. During the investigation, she encounters two female police detectives, and one—named Martinez—is played by Eva Longoria. They work together to solve the mystery surrounding the death of Rios' brother. Produced by Breakaway Films, *Senorita Justice* was aimed at the Latino home video market.

Four years later, in 2008, while *Housewives* was in its prime, Eva appeared in a comedy called *Over Her Dead Body*. Starring opposite actor Paul Rudd, as Dr. Henry Mills, she plays his fiancée, Kate, who is killed by an ice sculpture just before the couple is supposed to marry. Unable to forget his fiancée, Henry finally goes to a psychic, Ashley Clark, who pretends to speak with the dead Kate and tells Henry that it is time to move forward with his life.

Eventually Ashley and Henry fall in love, but this upsets Kate who has been watching everything from on high after her death. She intervenes in the relationship, and Ashley and Henry finally break up. When Kate realizes that Henry is very unhappy with the break-up, she eventually manages to bring the couple back together again.

This film was similar to other popular Hollywood movies, where a main character has died but returns as a ghost. It also followed a familiar plotline—boy meets girl, boy loses girl, boy gets girl again: the story of Henry and Ashley.

That same year, Eva also appeared in a film titled *Lower Learning*. The story focuses on a poorly run urban school, Geraldine Ferraro Elementary School, where the students are failing. Longoria plays an inspector, sent in by the School Board, to gather evidence that will lead to shutting down the school. She finds that one of her former schoolmates, the vice principal, is trying

Without Men

In 2010, as the *Desperate Housewives* series neared its final season, Eva appeared in another low-budget film, *Without Men*, with co-star Christian Slater. The plot describes a Latin American village whose men are forced to join a local guerrilla group, leaving the women to run the community. Eva leads them as they try to hold their community together.

to improve the elementary school. Instead of working against him, Longoria tries to help him save the school.

Unfortunately for Eva, the film was panned by critics. One New York film reviewer, Neil Rosen gave it "one wormy apple," an award he reserved for movies that he thought were terrible.[1]

Greater Glory

In 2012, Eva starred in *For Greater Glory*, set in Mexico during the late 1920s. The film included a cast of well-known actors, such as Andy Garcia, Ruben Blades, and Peter O'Toole. The biggest budget film ever produced in Mexico, it was a step up for Longoria's film career.

The film describes the revolt of the Cristeros—strong supporters of the Catholic Church—against the Mexican government, which was trying to reduce the Church's power. Garcia plays the role of General Enrique

Longoria starred in the big-budget epic *For Greater Glory* in 2012. The movie was not seen by many, but Longoria received good reviews.

Gorostieta Velarde, leader of the Cristeros, while Eva Longoria stars as his wife. She tries to talk her husband out of leaving his retirement to take on the dangerous job of leading the Cristeros. Ruben Blades is the ruthless Mexican president who orders the murder of priests— including one played by O'Toole—in an effort to control the Church. In his review of the film and the eventual victory of the Cristeros, critic Roger Ebert wrote: "*For Greater Glory* is the kind of long, expensive epic not much made any more. It bears the hallmarks of being a labor of love. It is also very heavy on battle scenes, in which the Cristeros seem to have uncannily good aim.

But in its use of locations and sets, it's an impressive achievement...."[2]

Films to Forget and Remember

In 2013, Eva appeared in another film, *The Baytown Outlaws*. She had only a minor role, along with acclaimed film star, Billy Bob Thornton. They play a divorced couple battling over custody of their teenaged son, Rob. Longoria hires a group of outlaws to rescue Rob from Thornton, who has kidnapped him. But the film turned out to be a disappointment among filmgoers. The *Hollywood Reporter* said the film was a "grimy macho assault [that] is all attitude, no thrills. A barrage of unbelievable stereotypes try to kill each other in [the] dispiriting exploitation flick."[3]

At about the same time, Longoria appeared with stars Andy Garcia and Forest Whitaker in *A Dark Truth*, which tells the story of a group of rebels in Ecuador trying to avenge the massacre of villagers by the government. Government leaders are under the thumb of a wealthy Canadian company that directed the massacre to cover up unsafe practices that are polluting the water in the village. The rebels are led by Whitaker and his wife, played by Eva Longoria. Reviewer Frank Scheck wrote that "Garcia and Whitaker invest their characterizations with their customary gravitas, and Longoria...impressively matches their earnestness.[4]

Frontera

In 2014, Longoria starred in her first Spanish-speaking role, playing the pregnant wife of an illegal Mexican immigrant charged with murder. The film also starred Ed Harris as a sheriff whose wife, Olivia, is the victim of the crime. Longoria's character bravely decides to leave Mexico and illegally cross the border into Arizona to help her husband. Along the way, however, she must pay a ruthless coyote—the name for those who illegally transport immigrants across the American border—to bring her into the United States.

The subject of the movie *Frontera* mattered greatly to Longoria.

The Immigration Issue

For Longoria, *Frontera* was a film that dealt with issues close to her heart—the difficult and controversial questions surrounding immigration. Each year, more than 50,000 children try to cross the American border. Longoria stated: "Little is being done to understand who these children are, where they're coming from, what they're facing. They had the bad luck to be born in poor violent countries in Central America. These children are running for their lives, and they believe that the United States will protect them. And 'will we?' is the question, and I don't know."[5]

Film critic Sheri Linden wrote that although the decision by a pregnant woman who speaks no English to cross the border did not seem believable, "That's no fault of Longoria, who's convincingly determined, vulnerable and all but broken as a victim of a predatory coyote...."[6]

Longoria was the executive producer of the Hispanic-targeted series *Devious Maids*. She is shown here with cast member Ana Ortiz (left).

Chapter 10

WORKING IN TELEVISION

Eva's role in *Desperate Housewives* ended in 2012, but her involvement in television continued. During the next few years she made her mark as an actor, a producer, and a director.

In 2013, Longoria collaborated with producer Marc Cherry—the pair had worked together on *Housewives*—to create a series called *Devious Maids*. The comedy/drama show revolved around five Hispanic maids who work for Hollywood's rich and beautiful people.

It was a series similar to *Desperate Housewives*. And like that series, it involved a mystery because one of the maids was actually an undercover detective who is investigating the murder of a maid in one of the wealthy homes. Originally scheduled to be in the ABC fall lineup, it was picked up instead by the Lifetime network.

There were thirteen episodes in the first season, followed by the same number of shows in 2014 and 2015. Thirteen episodes is not considered a full season on television. Instead, *Devious Maids* was based on the telanovela concept—that is, a miniseries. Telenovelas have been popular for many years in Latin America, Southeast Asia, and Europe. Some are based on novels, while others are created especially for television. They are collectively known as Spanish soap operas.

Telenovelas

There are several genres of telenovelas. Those for adults include romantic comedies, working-class dramas, murder mysteries, and historical romance. Telenovelas for teens often center around pop bands, supernatural elements, or teen drama. Although telenovelas feature some styles and themes similar to soap operas, they differ in that they tell one self-contained story and therefore have a faster pace.

Some Hispanic viewers criticized the series, saying that it promoted stereotypes among Latinas—Hispanic women. A story in the *New York Times* stated, "There still hasn't been…a show that deals with Latino culture in a way that doesn't offend viewers with crude stereotypes." But Longoria defended the series. "Stereotypes are constructed and perpetuated by those who believe in them. I choose not to."[1]

Longoria not only served as producer of the show but also made her directing debut on one of the shows in 2014. The Latinas who appeared on *Devious Maids* make up the small number of Hispanic roles on television. While Hispanics are more than 15 percent of the American population, they make up only 4 percent of the characters portrayed in television programs.[2]

Other Television Ventures

Meanwhile, Eva had returned to television as an actress in several different programs. In 2014, she appeared as a defense attorney for three episodes of *Brooklyn Nine-Nine*, a comedy on the Fox Network. She also signed for a starring role in *Telenovela*, based on a popular Latin American soap opera, which is due to air in 2015. The series portrays the private and public life of a soap star, played by Longoria.

"There are few actresses with as much international appeal as Eva Longoria, " said NBC president Jennifer Salk. "She is a perfect fit for *Telenovela*. Her character will try to navigate the hysteria and high-jinks that everyone must endure in putting together a daily show."[3]

In other television ventures, however, Eva's efforts did not have the hoped-for results. Her TV dating competition series, *Ready for Love*, was canceled after only a few episodes had aired on NBC. It had been appearing at 10 P.M., prime time in television. However, the series began on April 9, 2013 with only 3.8 million viewers, and continued declining in viewership.[4]

In 2013, Eva supplied the voice of a Latina Mom in the animated series, *Mother Up!* "She's a high-powered music exec that has quit her job and moved to the suburbs to become the mom she thinks she can be, and thinks her business skills will transfer over to parenting

Longoria works hard to hone her skills, attending professional development events such as the 7th Annual Produced By Conference.

skills" Longoria explained. "She doesn't understand why it won't transfer." Eva added that she also took the role because "there's no female presence in animation."[5]

However, reviewer Denise Wilson panned the show because the main character, Rudi, was too stiff and the show wasn't funny. *Mother Up!*'s only redeeming quality," Wilson added, "is Longoria herself, who has a voice tailor-made for animation. She deserves better than the oh-so-flawed Rudi, who is short on charm, while Longoria oozes it."[6] Longoria may play Rudi in *Mother Up!* but she admits that there is little similarity between them. "There's nothing I derive [draw] from to play her," she explained. "It's nice to play somebody that's totally different than me. She's narcissistic, she's selfish; everything roots from 'How does it best serve me?'"[7]

Food Chains, a documentary produced by Eva Longoria, focused on migrant farm workers.

Chapter 11

FOOD CHAINS

Many of Eva Longoria's film and television projects have provided opportunities for her and other Latino/Latina actors to expand the types of roles that they can play on screen. In addition, Eva has also been involved with films that expose the difficult lives that many Hispanic Americans are forced to endure in the United States.

In 2014, Longoria was executive producer of a documentary film called *Food Chains* that portrayed the lives of migrant farm workers living in Florida. Many Americans like to focus on what they eat—whether it's healthy, slimming, or organic. But as Eva reminded them in the documentary, "Everybody should be concerned with where our food comes from and who picks it."[1]

According to Cornell University, "Between 1 and 3 million migrant farm workers leave their homes every year to plant, cultivate, harvest and pack fruits, vegetables and nuts in the U.S. Although invisible to most people, the presence of migrant farm workers in many rural communities throughout the nation is undeniable, since hand labor is still necessary for the production of the blemish-free fruits and vegetables that consumers demand."[2]

The majority of migrant workers come from Mexico, just the way Eva Longoria's ancestors did. About one half of these workers are illegal immigrants. They leave Mexico and other Latin American countries because there are too few jobs. And they come to the United States, hoping to earn enough money to send home to their families so they can enjoy better lives.

Longoria is interested in shedding light on the difficult conditions endured by the migrant workers who harvest the food we eat.

While pay is better in the United States, the average income for most migrant workers is less than $7,500 per year.[3] Many are young, averaging about 30, and while some men come alone, others travel north with their families—both wives and children. Often entire families work together in the fields for 10 to 12 hours per day. And the work is backbreaking—bending down continually to pick fruits and vegetables, digging the ground with hoes to plant new crops, and dealing with pesticides that protect the plants but can cause diseases in humans.

The Stars of *Food Chains*

Food Chains focuses on the farm workers in southern Florida, specifically those who work on the tomato farms. Many of them live in appalling conditions inside labor camps. According to Jessica Floum, a reporter for the *Gainesville Sun,* workers at one camp had to cope with a septic system that "backed up, the commodes broke and burners on the stove leaked. Holes in the walls and windows without screens let in vicious summer bugs. The plumbing in one trailer leaked underneath it for days."[4]

Workers, as many as 35,000 in Florida, are often forced to live in these places because rents are low and they can't afford anything more. Each morning, the workers awake very early to board a bus that takes them from the camps to the fields where they work until dark, before being driven home.

Food Chains shines a light on these workers, mainly those who work on the tomato farms in Immokalee, Florida. The film premiered late in 2014, narrated by actor Forest Whitaker. It includes interviews with Longoria, activist Robert F. Kennedy Jr., and Delores Huerta.

Huerta was the co-founder of the United Farm Workers Union and worked side-by-side with co-founder Caesar Chavez to improve working conditions for migrant farm workers. Using strikes, boycotts, and political action, the UFW succeeded in raising pay rates from under $2 per hour in the 1960s to $6 per hour in the 1980s. Today that pay rate is higher but often amounts to less than the minimum wage.

According to Immokalee farm worker Gerardo Reyes Chavez, "Right now, a worker has to pick two and a quarter

Most migrant workers must put the whole family to work, including young children who toil long hours for little pay.

tons of tomatoes per day to make the equivalent of the minimum wage, and that's in an average day of 10 hours."[5]

"Food Chains" describes the efforts of the Fair Food Program created by the Coalition of Immokalee Workers (CIW) to change this situation. The program calls for a one cent increase in the price of tomatoes at supermarkets. This would have the effect of doubling the wages of migrant workers.

However, large supermarket chains want low prices to satisfy consumers. Large fast food chains like McDonald's also want to keep their prices low. But the coalition has persuaded McDonald's, Walmart, and Yum Brands (which owns Pizza Hut, KFC, and Long John Silver's) among others to sign on to a price rise as well as a guarantee of safe working conditions. The CIW battled for 13 years before Walmart finally agreed. However, other large chains like Wendy's, and supermarkets like Safeway, Publix and Kroger are still holding out.[6]

Indeed, part of *Food Chains* describes the battle against Publix, including a six day hunger strike at the supermarket chain's headquarters. This battle is continuing as the CIW tries to achieve higher wages for farm workers. *Food Chains*, which has been shown throughout the United States, was an effort to bring this fight to the public's attention.

During her on-camera interview in *Food Chains*, Eva Longoria said, "Grocery store prices are at an all-time high. It's despicable that farm worker wages are below the poverty line."[7]

Eva Longoria put her love of food and cooking into a book of recipes titled *Eva's Kitchen: Cooking With Love for Family and Friends* in 2011.

Chapter 12

COOKING WITH EVA

"My love affair with cooking started long ago, but I remember it so clearly. When I was about six years old, my mom was leaving for work and I told her I was hungry. 'So cook something,' she answered. ...I selected the smallest frying pan I could find, because I wanted to cook one egg. Not eggs, just one egg. I cracked the egg on the edge of the pan as I'd seen my mom do effortlessly many times before, and emptied it into the frying pan. Of course, the pan was full of eggshell. I didn't use any butter or oil so the egg got stuck everywhere. I cannot even remember now what the egg tasted like. But I can recall the feeling of accomplishment after cooking that egg. I found it empowering and energizing. I was hooked from that day forward."[1]

This is the beginning of Eva Longoria's cookbook, *Eva's Kitchen: Cooking with Love for Family and Friends*, which was published in 2011. The book includes sections with recipes for Appetizers, Soups and Salads, Beef Main Courses, Poultry Main Courses, Tortillas, Desserts as well as Drinks, among other recipes and anecdotes.

Eva recalled that she was influenced by her mother, a great cook. Her father did not believe in fast food eating, so they cooked all their meals at home. There was a garden with fresh vegetables outside that provided some of the ingredients for the dishes at each meal. Then there was Eva's Aunt Elsa, "A vault of recipes lay at the tip of her tongue," Eva writes.[2]

Aunt Elsa had a catering business, so she knew how to cook for large groups and intimate family gatherings. She also knew how to beautifully present food at the table. "Every day she had a cooking tip for me and she always volunteered it unasked."[3] Eva dedicated her cookbook to Aunt Elsa who gave lessons to everyone in the family on the art of preparing good food.

The cookbook also grew out of important Longoria family traditions. Whenever someone got married, the family would collect recipes, create a cookbook, and give it to the bride so she would know how to cook for her family. One of these recipes was for perfect Mexican rice because Eva's family believed that a bride who knew how to cook rice was ready to marry.

Eva's book contains recipes with a Mexican heritage as well as French and American and Latin American influences. And, as Eva explains, the kitchen is her favorite place to be, not only because she cooks there. It is also a place where friends and family gather while she

Remembering the People Who Provide Our Food

In the introduction to her cookbook, Eva also took an opportunity to remember those people who pick the fruits and vegetables that make up the recipes she included. One way to help these people, she explains, is to buy organic food. This food is not treated with the dangerous pesticides that can cause diseases among farm workers. "Buy organic produce. Switching over to even a minimal amount of organic produce means that you are supporting producers whose workers do not handle and inhale the powerful pesticides that conventional farms use regularly."[4]

is cooking to share in conversation, reminisce about the past, and prepare good things to eat.

For example, the Appetizer section includes goat cheese balls, hot artichoke dip, Dad's shrimp cocktail, chunky guacamole with serrano peppers, and avocado stuffed shrimp. It's a group of mouthwatering selections, complete with a list of ingredients, steps to follow in preparing the dishes, and beautiful pictures.

As renowned chef Mario Batali wrote, "Eva's recipes are simple, delicious, and enticing, and they form a perfect bridge between down-home Texas, Latin zing, and easy-to-make perfection. I'd be happy to eat the spicy stuff in Eva's kitchen every day."[5] The critics agreed. "Viva Eva!! wrote one reviewer. Oh my ... this cookbook is great. Being Hispanic, growing up in Texas, these

Longoria with famed chef Todd English at their popular Los Angeles restaurant Beso.

recipes remind me of my childhood. As Eva describes each recipe with love they are amazing. … Buy this book … learn the recipes … you will never go out for Mexican food again."[6]

The book not only presents Eva's recipes, but intertwines stories from her life. These include her childhood in Texas, her vacations in the United States and abroad, dinners with friends, and Hollywood pre-party specials. She drew on recipes from restaurants in Florence, Italy, and Normandy, France.

The image that Eva presented in her cookbook was far different from the Gabrielle Solis who appeared for eight years in *Desperate Housewives*. Nevertheless, Eva as a cook and homemaker are also key elements of Longoria's personality, and an essential part of her cultural inheritance.

Longoria spoke to delegates at the 2012 Democratic National Convention.

Chapter 13

POLITICAL ACTIVIST

In September 2012, Eva Longoria appeared before the delegates at the Democratic National Convention that had assembled to nominate President Barack Obama for a second term. In her speech, Longoria criticized the Republican nominee, Mitt Romney, for caring only about the rich, not the millions of Americans struggling financially.

"The Eva Longoria who worked at Wendy's flipping burgers—she needed a tax break. But the Eva Longoria who works on movie sets does not."[1] During the presidential election, Longoria co-chaired the President's campaign in California. Obama won that state in November 2012 and was overwhelmingly re-elected, receiving the vast majority of Hispanic votes on his way to a second term as president.

At the celebrations for the President's second inauguration in January 2013, Eva Longoria was a glamorous presence at the inaugural balls in Washington.

Reporter Philip Sherwell called her "Obama's newest Hispanic political power chip ... playing an increasingly serious part in American public life: using her profile to push for greater recognition of the contribution made by the country's largest minority, to culture, the economy and to politics."[2]

Longoria served as co-chair of the President's inaugural committee because of her campaign work during the election. She also sat on the platform in Washington, D.C., along with the President, First Lady Michelle Obama, and the Obama family for the President's Second Inaugural Address.

Eva is a strong supporter of the President's 2014 initiative to offer a route to citizenship for the children of millions of illegal immigrants. And she hosted a Washington gathering for a group of Democrats and Republicans to work together on immigration and other issues. She believes that Republicans may support immigration reform. "I think Republicans are going to realize, if they don't do it because it's morally imperative, they have to do it because it's politically imperative," Longoria explained.[3] In other words, with the number of Hispanic Americans and Hispanic voters growing year after year, Republicans must try to appeal to them or lose much of their power in politics. As Longoria put it, "We all went through the bruising [presidential] campaign together and we were all very loyal to our parties, to our candidates, but now it's time to be loyal to America." To help burnish her credentials in politics and

Longoria worked tirelessly for President Barack Obama's 2012 reelection. She recognized the importance of the Latino vote.

as a spokesperson for Hispanic groups, Longoria had already returned to college to earn a Master's Degree in Chicana and Chicano Studies. She has been a staunch supporter of the Democratic Party because President Obama has taken the lead on immigration reform. As one political activist put it, "Eva is the real deal, very authentic. Unlike a lot of Hollywood celebrities, her political activity is not just checking the box [voting]. She has blue collar roots, she's passionate about issues and she does her homework."[4]

Graduate Degree

In May 2013, Eva graduated with a Master's Degree in Chicana and Chicano Studies from California State University Northridge. "Big Day today!!!" she tweeted. "Very excited to graduate for my Master's degree in Chicano Studies. You're never too old or too busy to continue your education!"[5]

Latino Victory Project

Longoria also recognized how important it is for other Latinos to become actively involved in politics. In the 2012 presidential election as about 50 percent of Latinos voted, President Obama received almost three quarters of their votes. But in midterm elections for Congress, less than one third of Latinos turned out to vote.

In 2014, Longoria helped to found the Latino Victory Project, which is aimed at encouraging more Latinos to go to the polls and vote. "We can't, as a community, be so engaged in the presidential elections and elect the president, but not turn up at midterms to elect the people who have to work with the President," Longoria said.[6] So far, Latinos are underrepresented in Congress. Only 28 Congressional representatives out of 435 and three Senators out of 100 are Hispanic.

"During the 2012 elections, we got a taste of how powerful the Latino community could be," Longoria said, "as record numbers of voters and donors participated in the political process. When we engage, we get a seat at the table." In her appearance before the group in 2014, Longoria was joined by co-founder Henry Munoz III, finance chairman of the Democratic National Committee, as well as the president of the Project, Representative Joaquin Castro of Texas.[7]

Meanwhile, Longoria has also been seriously considered for political office. She is a friend of President Obama's. She has worked with billionaire Warren Buffett's son to distribute millions of dollars in small loans to Latino business owners, and she has discussed Latino economic power with former President Bill Clinton.

In Texas, she has become a leading Latino force across the state in Democratic politics. "She would be a very strong candidate for statewide office," explained Texas Democratic chairman Gilberto Hinojosa. "I'd love to have her run for governor." But as Longoria knows, Latinos must vote in elections other than presidential contests for her to have a chance to win.[8]

The beautiful and intelligent Longoria has dated a wide variety of men, including actor Nicholas Gonzalez.

Chapter 14

HOLLYWOOD CELEBRITY

Eva Longoria is news. Fans want to know "Who is she dating?" "What is she wearing?" "Where is she appearing?" "How much is she worth?" "When will she star in another film or television program?" That's what it means to be a celebrity.

In an answer to the first question often asked by Eva's fans, she was dating singer Eduardo Cruz in 2011 and 2012. Cruz is the younger brother of actress Penelope Cruz. The couple met at a party and later spent time together on a yacht in Florida and later celebrated Eva's thirty-sixth birthday. But in March 2012, the couple split up.

Later that year, Eva began dating professional football quarterback Mark Sanchez for a while. During 2012, the couple were often seen in New York where Sanchez was quarterback for the New York Jets. But in the fall of that year, Sanchez and Longoria split up. A spokesperson for Sanchez said, explaining the breakup, "Mark adores and respects Eva. It really was about scheduling, more than anything. They will remain close friends." [1] In other words, both were so busy with their own schedules—Sanchez on the road playing for the Jets and Eva working in Hollywood—that they did not have time left to see each other. Another problem seemed to be the difference in their ages. Sanchez was 25 and Eva was more than ten years older.[2]

While Eva continued dating, there was apparently no serious relationship until she met Jose Antonio Bastion. He is the President of South America's largest media conglomerate, Televisa. In August 2014, the couple were photographed in Mexico City sharing lunch. According to *Daily Mail* reporter Julie Moult, "Eva, 39, smiled as she gazed lovingly at handsome multi-millionaire, Jose." A bachelor, Bastion was 45. Later on the *Ellen DeGeneres Show*, Eva talked about Bastion. "He's a good dresser. I always have to step it up. It's exhausting," she added jokingly.[3]

In another interview, Longoria added her thoughts on turning forty in 2015. "Age is something you can't control, so why worry about it. I would never want to repeat my 20s. I welcome age with open arms because I want to evolve as a human being, gain more wisdom. I have so much more to do! And the only way you do that is with age." Speaking about Bastion, Longoria added: "I am attracted to humor and intellect in a man. Let me tell you, I'm very lucky in my life." According to *People* magazine, Bastion was "sweeping [her] off her feet and courting her like a proper gentleman."[4]

However, Longoria also admitted that she was not interested in having children. "It's not in my future. It is not on the horizon right now so it's not something I think about." Nevertheless, she still enjoys working with children. "With kids, I love their energy and spirit and innocence."[5]

Fashion and Glamour

Eva Longoria is considered one of the most beautiful stars in Hollywood. And she appears on the covers of numerous fashion magazines. She stays in great physical shape because "I run a lot. I'm a big runner. And I do yoga. So, I just alternate. Run, yoga, run, yoga. I do weight training as well."[6]

In 2014, for example, Eva was selected as *Maxim* magazine's Woman of the Year. The cover of the magazine featured her with a scanty costume, followed by more photos inside. "It's especially awesome," Eva said, "after how long it's been since my first cover. I've had a beautiful relationship with *Maxim* over all these years." Previously in 2005 and 2006 she had been selected as one of the magazine's Hot 100.

"One thing people are usually surprised about when they get to know me is how domestic I am," she added. "So when you see the sexy *Maxim* cover and then you put it against me in an apron with flour in my hair, it takes a moment to reconcile that image."[7]

In addition, Eva has also appeared on the cover of other fashion magazines. In 2009, for example, she appeared in *Prestige Magazine,* based in Hong Kong.

Net Worth

Eva Longoria's net worth is estimated at $35 million. She has earned this money herself, starring in television programs, including eight years in *Desperate Housewives*. She has also appeared in numerous films and she has been featured on the cover of many fashion magazines. She earned $1.3 million in the last year of *Desperate Housewives*.

She also appeared on the cover of *Latina* magazine in October 2014. In that magazine, Longoria said, "People go, 'How does it feel to be so successful?' and I always think…I haven't even tapped my potential as a human being." "I think people go, 'Oh, you like politics and politicians?' And I say I don't like politics and I don't like politicians, but I love the political process."[8] In addition, Eva appeared on the cover of *Vogue Mexico*, in January 2015. In addition, she makes frequent appearances on television talk shows, in an effort to keep her name and her face in front of the public. One way she accomplished this goal has been by signing a contract to appear as a model for L'Oreal makeup. L'Oreal features Longoria as a cover girl in its advertisements, increasing her name recognition. In November 2014, she also shared some of her beauty secrets with *Glamour* magazine.

Back to Her Roots

But her work with *Glamour* did not stop there. She also appeared in a documentary called *A Path Appears*, based

Although Longoria appears on magazine covers and enjoys cosmetic endorsements, not all of her pursuits are related to her beauty.

on a book by *New York Times* columnist Nicholas Kristof and Sheryl WuDunn. The documentary investigated poverty in the United States and South America, focusing especially on the factors behind gender inequality.

Longoria went to Cartagena, Colombia to focus on an important reason why girls drop out of school and live in poverty. "Every step we took, there was another pregnant child, and none of them were in class," she said in the film. It was epidemic. Sometimes the only way to help," she added "is one neighborhood at a time, one family at a time, one girl at a time."[9]

Longoria's commitment to people in the larger Latino community is never far from her thoughts. Whether she is involved in politics, producing documentaries, or social activism, Eva has tried to ensure that those who have been less fortunate than she are given every opportunity to lead satisfying lives.

Chapter 15

DIET, EXERCISE, AND BEAUTY SECRETS

Eva Longoria's physical appearance and her beauty are part of her images. She believes in staying thin. Eva weighs just over 100 pounds on a five foot two inch frame and wears a size zero dress. But she does not advocate staying too thin.

That's what happened to her during her divorce from Tony Parker. Her weight dropped because, Eva admitted, she was depressed. And her diet consisted mainly of drinking coffee. "People kept saying, 'You look amazing. Divorce agrees with you.' And I was like, 'I don't feel good. I have no energy.' I didn't know I was depressed. I mean, I knew it was a sad moment in my life, but I wouldn't categorize myself as depressed. . . . I was not eating, I was sad."[1]

Finally, Longoria made an appointment with her doctor who explained that she had a severe iron deficiency and her liver was not functioning properly. "… so I had to saturate with vitamins and kind of get back onto…track."[2]

Eva Longoria's usual diet, when she is not sad or depressed, is usually right on track. For breakfast, she has a protein-rich meal consisting of egg whites or fruit, which is high in fiber. Lunch might be chicken with a salad. Fruits as well as vegetables—another favorite of Eva's—are low in calories and give you the feeling of being full so you do not crave more food. "I'm not obsessed with my diet," says Eva. "I love fish and vegetables, but I love my cheeseburgers and pizza. Everything in moderation is fine."[3] Eva's favorite vegetables include spinach and brussel sprouts. She also enjoys yogurt and nuts. But she tries to stay away as much as possible from foods that are high in carbohydrates and prefers lean protein, found in fish or lean meat. Her major rule is to eat everything in moderation, which helps Eva maintain her weight and slim figure. This also makes her look young even in her forties. "It's just dieting. I don't really eat a lot of sugar. My diet usually consists of no sugar, no carbs, and then I workout…."[4]

Eva's Workouts

While her diet helps keep her thin, Eva also exercises regularly. She usually works out three times per week, following a similar routine during each workout. Usually she works with a trainer. She says this helps her keep to a routine. Other people might prefer to exercise on their own following a healthy and safe routine. And students

Working out with a mix of cardio, strength training, and yoga keeps Longoria in excellent physical and mental health.

should probably consult a physical education teacher or coach before starting their exercise program.

Her workout begins with ten minutes of aerobic exercises, like running on a treadmill or pedaling a stationary bicycle. Then she does a variety of stretching and muscle building exercises to help her body keep fit. Eva varies the exercises so that she will not become bored, by simply spending an hour on the treadmill or bicycle.

For example, she does a series of exercises designed to strengthen her legs, such as dumbbell lunges and jump squats. A jump squat starts by squatting down, with your back straight and your eyes looking forward; and then jumping up as high as possible with your hands reaching upward. A more advanced form of the jump squat includes holding a dumbbell in each hand while doing the exercise.

Longoria strengthens her arms by doing exercises such as triceps extensions and bicep curls. For a triceps extension, you can begin by lying on your back on the floor, and holding a small dumbbell in each hand. Next raise your elbows so the dumbbells are over your chest. Then extend your arms until the dumbbells are level with your forehead. Finally, extend your elbows, straighten your arms, and go back to the position at the beginning of the exercise.

Eva also does a series of workouts that are designed to keep her abdomen as flat as possible. These include bicycle crunches and reverse crunches. A reverse crunch

Alternate Method of Triceps Extension

Sit on a chair with a dumbbell in each hand.

Lift both dumbbells over your head.

Lower your forearms behind the upper arms by flexing your elbows.

Flex and extend your wrists.

Return to the original position and repeat the exercise.

begins by lying on your back on the floor or a mat, with one hand on each side of each hip. Then slowly lift your hips off the ground, keeping your knees bent. Lower your hips back onto the floor. Repeat the exercise until your abdomen begins to tighten.

Eva studied kinesiology at the University of Texas, where she became familiar with routines to keep her body as fit as possible. She also worked for a time as a physical trainer. So Longoria is no stranger to how to keep herself fit, a more difficult task as the body ages. She believes that ten minutes or so doing aerobic exercises—those that raise the heartbeat and rate of breathing—followed by muscle strengthening are an effective approach for anyone wanting to stay in shape. You can also add push-ups—another of Eva's favorites.

Moderate eating habits are also a key. This means only small amounts of sugar and carbohydrates. These leave you feeling unsatisfied a few minutes later, so you continue to eat. Moderation also means no binge eating—pushing in large amounts of candy and cookies while washing these down with sugary drinks. This only leads to being overweight and eventual obesity.

Eva's Beauty Secrets

Eva Longoria is considered one of America's most beautiful women. And she has retained her beauty into the decades when many begin to fade. Most of her beauty secrets are fairly simple, but by regularly using them, Eva ensures that her face will always attract attention.

For example, as she was attending the international Cannes Film Festival in France, she talked about her skin rituals. Most importantly, these included applying moisturizers each night to her face along with Vitamin C and various beauty creams.[5]

In an interview with *Hello* magazine in 2012, Eva was asked, "What's your biggest beauty secret?" Her answer: "Moisturizing. Because I fly so much, hydration is important. When you have good skin, everything else kind of falls into place. Also, I use blush with shimmer in it. That way, your skin glows and people notice it."[6]

When asked about her most important makeup products, Longoria explained: "Firstly, mascara. Ever since doing the [film] shoot for [a mascara product] I have become addicted. I love the brush and the texture of mascara. It's not clumpy and is the blackest black. Then all I would need is a bronzer and some fresh water."[7] "During the day I apply moisturizer and bronzer all over, then mascara—and that's it. I am ready," Eva explained. "I rarely blow-dry my hair because it is naturally wavy and I can't be bothered. I color my hair so much—and prefer being a dark brunette as it's natural and effortless—but I always use sulphate-free shampoos and conditioners to keep the color."[8] She also adds blonde highlights. One beauty item that travels everywhere with Eva is her tweezers. "I am obsessed with plucking my eyebrows," she admits. "I always end up doing them on a plane at 30,000 feet because the light is so good."[9] In 2012, Eva introduced her own perfume, called EVAmour. "My first memory of fragrance is my mom," she explained. "I would always sneeze when I smelled it and just never found one that worked for me, which is why I wanted to develop my own … playful, sexy and mature." The perfume combines bergamot, with apple, red current, vanilla, amber, and musk. Longoria contacted a perfume manufacturer, explained the smell she wanted and spent a year developing it.[10]

Makeup

For Eva, being a Hollywood star has its pluses and minuses. For example, she has to wear a great deal of makeup for photo shoots in magazine advertisements, magazine covers, and film appearances. "I can't wait to get it off when I get home," Eva explains. And this is the reason she has a "nightly routine" with her moisturizers, vitamin C, and lip balm. Asked if she would rather be natural or made up, Longoria admits that she'd rather be natural. "But I love and appreciate getting glammed

Although she's happiest when she's natural, Eva Longoria can do glamour extremely well.

up. I think it's a privilege to be on the red carpet [at Hollywood galas with lots of press]; most women get to do it a few times in their life—their prom, wedding—but I experience it weekly."[11]

"My makeup artist," Longoria continues, "taught me about the importance of blending. She really works the base in and blends colors—shadows, blush, so when people ask me what shade I'm wearing, I'm always like, 'about ten different things.'"[12] Eva also wears false eyelashes. "That's been my beauty tip since my pageant days."[13]

Eva Longoria has come a long way since her beauty pageant appearances in Texas. Then the pageant judges noticed her poise, face, and figure. But as she matured, Longoria exhibited the native smarts that earned her a college diploma, and a Master's degree. She has also known how to manage her career very successfully from bit parts in television programs and films, to stardom on *Desperate Housewives*.

Eva has always recognized how to keep herself in front of the public, keep herself looking glamorous, and physically fit. These have all been important parts of a successful career. They have also enabled her to develop an Eva Longoria brand that is a symbol for glamour, beauty, and intelligence.

Longoria uses her celebrity and influence to help call attention to a variety of people in need.

Chapter 16

In 2015, Eva Longoria was named Harvard University Artist of the Year, by the Harvard Foundation—its most important art award. Director of the Foundation, S. Allen Counter, said, "Our student committee praised her outstanding contributions to the performing arts and her much-admired humanitarian work through Eva's Heroes, a charity founded by Longoria that helps developmentally disabled children, as well as her support of the National Center for Missing and Exploited Children," an organization that tries to prevent the abduction and exploitation of children. Other performing artists who have won this prestigious honor in the past include actors Andy Garcia, Salma Hayek, and Queen Latifah as well as jazz great, Quincy Jones.[1]

In many ways, the award from Harvard University seemed to symbolize and sum up what the forty-year-old actress had been trying to achieve throughout her life. Not only had she dedicated herself to the craft of acting, but also to the goal of making life better for other people. To a large degree, both of these endeavors define Eva Longoria.

Her public career began in the 1990s, winning a beauty pageant in Corpus Christi, Texas. For many beauty queens, however, awards begin and end with a single victory, and they are never heard from again. But Longoria did not stop there. She turned that success into a Hollywood career. At first, there were small, undemanding parts in television soap operas and unsuccessful films.

Once again, this is as far as many actors seem to go. But Longoria did not stop there. Through hard work, acting skill, and her contacts in Hollywood, she finally achieved the breakthrough that comes only to a relative handful of actors—stardom. This was an eight-year run as Gabrielle Solis on *Desperate Housewives*. This opportunity also enabled Eva to become a multimillionaire.

Once again, Eva might have been content and stopped there. But she successfully managed her career into more films, television programs, talk-show appearances, and a multitude of photo opportunities on the covers of international fashion magazines.

This required hard work. Eva dedicated herself to staying in shape: working out regularly and following a careful diet to stay thin, youthful looking, and beautiful as she turned forty.

Throughout all of these accomplishments, Eva never forgot her roots. She always remembered who she was and where she had come from. Longoria is a Latina from a Mexican-American family that traced its roots as far back as fifteenth century Spain. She wrote a cookbook, featuring her Mexican-American recipes. She also produced documentaries, like *The Harvest* and *Food Chains,* which focused on the plight of migrant farm workers—men, women, and children who are overwhelmingly Hispanic immigrants.

ESPN

In 2015, Longoria produced a series of short films for ESPN. The first in the series, called *VERSUS,* focuses on Sebastien De La Cruz, a mariachi singer from San Antonio. He sang the "Star Spangled Banner" at game 3 of the NBA Championship series in 2013. "I really wanted to tell that story because what came out of it was something beautiful...and what it's about to be Mexican," she explained.[2] Another film features Violet Palmer, the first female referee in the NBA.

Just as important, Eva Longoria turned her talents to political activism. While she admitted to not enjoying politics, she did believe in the political process and knew what it could accomplish. Activism earlier in the twentieth century by Latino and Latina leaders,

Most people consider her a success story, but Eva Longoria believes she hasn't yet tapped her potential as a human being.

like Cesar Chavez and Dolores Huerta, had helped to achieve important civil rights for Hispanic Americans. Activism had also enabled migrant workers to obtain higher wages and better working conditions.

Eva recognized that Hispanics comprised the fastest growing segment of the American population—one that could wield significant political power in state and national elections. So she campaigned for Democrats, including President Barack Obama, who seemed sympathetic to the needs of American minority groups. She also broke into the upper echelon of Democratic Party politics.

In short, Eva Longoria has made sure that her life has made a difference. This is an important achievement for anyone—especially for someone who started from modest circumstances as Eva did in 1975. From flipping hamburgers at a fast food restaurant, Longoria worked her way up the ladder of success until she had fulfilled a position that many might find enviable. But it did not happen because of her family name or because they possessed great wealth that opened so many doors for her.

It happened because Eva Longoria never stopped trying to make outstanding contributions as an artist and humanitarian.

Chronology

1975—Eva Longoria is born in Corpus Christi, Texas.

1993—Graduates from Roy Miller High School, and enters Texas A&M University, Kingsville.

1998—Crowned Miss Corpus Christi.

1999—Appears on *L.A. in a Day.*

2000—Appears in *Beverly Hills, 90210.*

2001–2003—Appears in *The Young and the Restless.*

2002—Marries Tyler Christopher.

2003–2004—Stars in *Dragnet.*

2004–2012—Stars as Gabrielle Solis in *Desperate Housewives.*

2003—Longoria begins a long association with *PADRES.*

2004—Stars in *Senorita Justice.* Divorces from Tyler Christopher.

2006—Longoria founds *Eva's Heroes.* Appears in *The Sentinel.*

2007—Marries Tony Parker.

2008—Appears in *Over Her Dead Body.* Stars in *Lower Learning.*

2009—Divorces Tony Parker.

2010—Appears in *Without Men..*

2011—Longoria produces *The Harvest.* Publishes

Eva's Kitchen: Cooking with Love for Family and Friends.

2012—Stars in *For Greater Glory.* Co-chaired President Obama's reelection campaign in California.

2013—Appears in *The Baytown Outlaws* and *A Dark Truth.* Produces *Devious Maids* and *Ready for Love.* Earns Master's degree in Chicano and Chicana Studies.

2014—Stars in *Frontera,* guest stars in *Brooklyn Nine-Nine,* and signs for starring role in *Telenovela.* Produces *Food Chains.* Becomes co-founder of *Latino Victory Project.* Appears in *A Path Appears.*

Chapter Notes

CHAPTER 1. A CELEBRATION

1. Empty, "The Hollywood Reporter Honors Eva Longoria Parker, " Associated Press, November 15, 2009.
2. "Eva Longoria to Host PADRES Contra El Cancer's 14th Annual El Sueno De Esperanza, 'Look to the Stars,'" October, 2014.
3. Lucy Hood, "Documentary Review: The Harvest," AARP VIVA, June 30, 2011.
4. Ibid.
5. Ibid.
6. Ibid.

CHAPTER 2. CORPUS CHRISTI ROOTS

1. Russell Contreras, "Corpus Christi, Texas, a destination for Latino History," Associated Press, April 19, 2013.
2. James Pylant and Paula Lane Corregan, "Eva Longoria: The Roots of a Desperate Housewife," Genealogy Magazine.com, 2007.
3. "Eva Longoria," Faces of America, with Henry Louis Gates, Jr., PBS, 2010.
4. Ibid.
5. Sarah Tressler, "Heroes is Built on Family Values," *San Antonio Express-News*, November 28, 2013.

CHAPTER 3. THE BIG BREAK

1. Mike Bratten, "Eva Longoria Finds Opportunities Everywhere These Days," *Corpus Christi Caller-Times*, August 10, 1998.
2. Ibid.
3. Ibid.

CHAPTER 4. TELEVISION ACTRESS

1. Sheri Stritof, "Eva Longoria and Tyler Christopher Marriage Profile," http://marriage.about.com/od/entertainmen1/p/tylereva.htm, 2007.

2. Ibid.

3. "Eva Longoria," People.com, http://www.people.com/people/eva_longoria, January 16, 2015.

CHAPTER 5. STARDOM

1. Eva Longoria's post, "It's Confirmed…." *WhoSay*, August 7, 2011.

2. Bauder, David, "ABC's 'Housewives' Starts," *Boston Globe*, September 20, 2013.

3. "Gabrielle Solis," ABC.com, http://abc.go.com/shows/desperate-housewives/cast/character-gabrielle-solis.

4. "Eva Longoria," http://people.com/eva_Longoria, January 16, 2015.

CHAPTER 6. THE SUCCESS OF *DESPERATE HOUSEWIVES*

1. "You Magazine," *British Daily Mail,* September 2006.

CHAPTER 7. A PUBLIC AND PRIVATE LIFE

1. "Interview with Eva Longoria," CBS News, June 11, 2006.

2. Ibid.

3. "You Magazine," *British Daily Mail,* September 2006.

4. "Tony Parker Biography," Jock Bio, http://www.jockbio.com/Bios/Parker/Parker_bio.html, 2013.

5. "Eva Longoria's First Words on Her Divorce," *Extra,* November 17, 2010.

6. "Eva Longoria's San Antonio Texas, Luxury Home," Home Luxury.net, http://www.homeluxury.net/eva-

longorias-san-antonio-texas-luxury-home/, May 28, 2011.

7. Arienne Thompson, "Eva Longoria Opens Up about Tony Parker Split," *USA Today,* May 11, 2012.

CHAPTER 8. GABRIELLE SOLIS: DESPERATE HOUSEWIFE

1. Bill Gorman, "complete List of 2011-2012 Season TV Show Viewership," *TV by the Numbers,* May 24, 2012.
2. Christiana Guppy, "ABC's Desperate Housewives: The Paint Colors of Wisteria Lane," *Hirshfield's,* 2006.
3. Ibid.
4. William Keck, "Behind the Scenes for Desperate Housewives' Emotional Series Finale," TV Guide. Com, http://www.tvguide.com/news/desperate-housewives-finale-scoop-1046793/, April 30, 2012.
5. Ibid.
6. Ibid.
7. Nellie Andreeva, "Desperate Housewives Stars Finalizing New Deals," *Deadline Hollywood,* April 11, 2011.

CHAPTER 9. EVA'S FILMS

1. "Lower Learning," *Variety,* October 10, 2008.
2. Roger Ebert, "For Greater Glory Movie Review," http://www.rogerebert.com/reviews/for-greater-glory-2012, May 30, 2012.
3. John DeFore, "The Baytown Outlaws," *Hollywood Reporter,* January 9, 2013.
4. Frank Scheck, "A Dark Truth: Film Review," *Hollywood Reporter,* January 5, 2013.
5. Carolina Moreno, "Eva Longoria Like You've Never Seen Her Before," *Huffington Post,* July 30, 2014.

6. Sheri Linden, "Frontera: Film Review," *Hollywood Reporter,* September 1, 2014.

CHAPTER 10. WORKING IN TELEVISION

1. Eric Deggans, "Producer Eva Longoria's Show 'Devious Maids' Debuts with Debate," *Tampa Bay Times,* June 16, 2013.
2. Ibid.
3. Lynette Rice, "Eva Longoria to Star in new NBC Comedy," People.com, http://www.people.com/article/eva-longoria-nbc-telenova-new-series, January 16, 2015.
4. Nina Terrero, "Eva Longoria's "Ready for Love" Canceled and Remaining Episodes Will Go Online," NBC Latino.com, April 27, 2013.
5. Denette Wilford, "'Mother Up!' Review: Thumbs Down for Eva Longoria Show," *Huffington Post,* January 21, 2014.
6. Ibid.
7. Ibid.

CHAPTER 11. *FOOD CHAINS*

1. *Food Chains,*" 2014.
2. Eduardo Gonzales, Jr., "Migrant Farm Workers: Our Nation's Invisible Population," Cornell University Cooperative Extension, August 1, 2013.
3. Ibid.
4. Jessica Floum, "State's Migrant Workers Often Forced to Live in Squalor," *Gainesville Sun,* February 7, 2015.
5. Soraya Nadia McDonald, "Eva Longoria and Eric Schlosser Take on Fairness for Farmworkers in 'Food Chains,'" *Washington Post,* November 20, 2014.

6. Erin Sullivan, "Food Chains, a Documentary about Florida Farmworkers, to Screen in Altamonte Springs," *Orlando Weekly,* November 19, 2014.

7. *Food Chains,* 2014.

CHAPTER 12. COOKING WITH EVA

1. Eva Longoria, *Eva's Kitchen: Cooking with Love for Family and Friends* (New York: Clarkson Potter, 2011).

2. Ibid.

3. Ibid.

4. Ibid.

5. Ibid.

6. Michael Delfin, "Amazon Review," April 7, 2011.

CHAPTER 13. POLITICAL ACTIVIST

1. Philip Sherwell, "Eva Longoria Is Obama's Newest Hispanic Political Power Chip," *Telegraph,* January 27, 2013.

2. Ibid.

3. Ibid.

4. Ibid.

5. Brittany Galla, "Eva Longoria Graduates with a Master's Degree in Chicano Studies," *Us Weekly,* May 22, 2013.

6. Serena Marshall, "Eva Longoria Starts Latino Political Group," ABC News, May 5, 2014.

7. Griselada Nevarez, "Eva Longoria's Group Looks to Help Latinos Build Political Power," VOXXI, http://voxxi.com/2014/05/05/eva-longorias-latinos-political-power/, May 5, 2014.

8. "The Political Inevitability of Eva Longoria," LaRaza.com, http://www.laraza.com/-political-inevitability-of-eva-longoria&timediff=0, May 15, 2014.

CHAPTER 14. HOLLYWOOD CELEBRITY

1. "Eva Longoria, Mark Sanchez Split after Three Months," *New York Daily News*, October 24, 2012.

2. Ibid.

2. Allison Takeda, "Eva Longoria 'Very Happy' With Boyfriend Jose Antonio Baston, Says 'He's a Good Dresser,'" *Us Weekly*, April 14, 2014.

4. Billy Farrell, "Eva Longoria Admires Beau Jose Antonio Baston's 'Humor and Intellect,'" *People*, March 29, 2014.

5. "Eva Longoria: No Kids for Me!," Gossip Center, http://www.gossipcenter.com/eva-longoria/eva-longoria-no-kids-me-1623566, June 15, 2014.

6. Ibid.

7. Esther Lee, "Eva Longoria Is Maxim's Woman of the Year 2014," *Us Weekly*, January 6, 2014.

8. Kelli Acciardo, "Eva Longoria is Latina Magazine's October 2014 Cover Star!," *Latina*, October 2014.

9. "Eva Longoria's Mission to Help Girls Get an Education," *Glamour*, December 2014.

CHAPTER 15. DIET, EXERCISE, AND BEAUTY SECRETS

1. "Eva Longoria's Weight Loss Post-Divorce Was Scary: 'I Was Not Eating. I Was Sad,'" *Huffington Post*, April 26, 2013.

2. Ibid.

3. Marish Gupta, "Eva Longoria Workout and Diet," Health Today, http://www.health-today.org/eva-longoria-workout-and-diet/, November 5, 2011.

4. "Red Carpet Confidential: Eva Longoria Reveals Her Diet Secrets and the Cheat Food That She 'Can't Put

Down,'" *OK Magazine,* http://okmagazine.com/get-scoop/eva-longoria-diet-secrets/, October 25, 2013.

5. Paula Conway, "Beauty Craves: Get Skin Like Eva Longoria!," *New York Daily News,* May 18, 2014.

6. "Mascara, Moisturizer and Making an Entrance: Eva Longoria Chats to HELLO," http://us.hello magazine.com/healthandbeauty/201206198388/eva-longoria-beauty-secrets/, June 19, 2012.

7. Ibid.

8. Ibid.

9. Ibid.

10. Heather Muir, "The *Allure* Beauty Diaries: Eva Longoria's Sexy Beauty Secrets," http://www.allure.com/beauty-trends/blogs/daily-beauty-reporter/2012/03/allure-beauty-diaries, March 23, 2012.

11. Ibid.

12. Ibid.

13. Ibid.

CHAPTER 16. VIVA EVA!

1. "Eva Longoria to Get 'Artist of the Year' Honor from Harvard University," *Fox News Latino,* February 16, 2015.

2. "Eva Longoria Turns Focus on Sports World in New ESPN Films," *New York Times,* January 7, 2015.

Glossary

activist—A person who fights for social change.

Anglo—Hispanic term for a white American.

blue collar—Relating to people who do manual work for a living.

boycott—Mass effort by workers to prevent customers from buying certain products.

Chicana or Chicano—Female or male of Mexican origin or descent.

immigration—Coming to live permanently in a foreign country.

kinesiology—Study of physical exercise and movement.

Latina or Latino—Female or male of Latin American origin for descent.

organic—Food that is raised without the use of growth hormones or antibiotics, or that is grown without the use of synthetic fertilizers, pesticides, and that is not genetically modified.

pageant—A form of entertainment that involves a procession of people in costumes.

migrant worker—An agricultural worker who travels from field to field.

red carpet—A long, narrow red carpet on which a distinguished visitor walks.

telenovela—Spanish soap opera that is a miniseries.

Further Reading

BOOKS

Espejo, Roman. *Migrant Workers*. Farmington Hills, Mich.: Greenhaven Press, 2015.

Longoria, Eva. *Eva's Kitchen: Cooking with Love for Family and Friends*. New York: Clarkson Potter, 2011.

Worth, Richard. *Hispanic America, 1950s to 1960s*. New York: Marshall Cavendish, 2010.

Worth, Richard. *Hispanic America, 1970s to 1980s*. New York: Marshall Cavendish, 2010.

WEB SITES

evalongoriafoundation.org/

The Eva Longoria Foundation supports Latinas through educational and entrepreneurial programs.

evasheroes.org

Eva's Heroes helps individuals with special needs integrate into the community.

MOVIES

Longoria, Eva, producer. *The Harvest*. 2011.

Longoria, Eva, producer. *Food Chains*. 2014.

Index